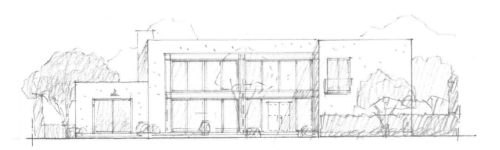

Patina Homes

Principal photography by
LISA ROMEREIN

Patina Homes

STEVE GIANNETTI & BROOKE GIANNETTI

GIBBS SMITH
TO ENRICH AND INSPIRE HUMANKIND

This book is dedicated to our clients,
who bring meaning to our work
by sharing their dreams with us
and trusting us to design their homes.

Thank you for inspiring others to
dream by allowing us to include your
private spaces in Patina Homes.

Introduction

My creative life began just outside of Washington, D.C., in my family's ornamental plaster studio, an environment that was equal parts classical and industrial. As a young boy, I spent my summers covered in a fine white dust, helping my father and paternal grandfather fabricate and install column capitals and other decorative architectural pieces, all the while learning about their historic meanings and the beauty they brought to these spaces.

Those summers of my youth were an opportunity to observe. I watched as the artisans carved the wooden molds that would be used over and over again to create the plaster ornament. I could see hints of their handwork in each finished piece. To this day, my designs reflect the respect I have for the craftsman's touch.

I also grew up appreciating the importance of palette. Being an industrial space, Giannetti Studio was built out of simple materials that were left unadorned. Wood and metal were in their natural states. As they aged, they developed a chalky "patina." This became the comforting, neutral backdrop of my childhood memories and is still what I prefer for my surroundings.

My experiences at Giannetti Studio shaped my image of ultimate beauty—a place where modern, classical and industrial elements merge to create a unique style with a modern sense of space and emotion drawn from history.

You will see these themes flow through all of the projects I share in *Patina Homes* and how I use these concepts to solve an array of architectural challenges, ultimately to create houses in a unique architectural style that also incorporates the stories and dreams of my clients.

My father's plaster studio near Washington, D.C.

11

LEFT: A collection of decorative plaster plaques, heads and medallions hang on a cement block wall in the stairway, inspiring plaster displays at our home, Patina Farm. ABOVE: A beautifully detailed plaster pineapple sits on top of an industrial lift at Giannetti Studio.

ABOVE: My father (far left) and grandfather (center) in the studio in 1961. It looked much the same then as it does today.
RIGHT: Craftsmen's work smocks hang on the door to the plaster drying room. The faded colors of the smocks and the aged patina of the wood-plank doors are the inspiration for our palette.

Patina Farm

Patina Farm is the result of my design collaboration with my wife, Brooke, and reflects the combination of our two unique stories and our shared dream. The architecture is both rustic and modern and was influenced by the history of its location in the small rural town of Ojai, California. For a year, we designed this five-acre property and imagined our life there while we took our morning walks, with the intention of creating a place that would appeal to like-minded future clients. Patina Farm is our "Field of Dreams," and we believed that if we built it, they would come.

Our intention was to create a timeless home that felt as if it had been built decades ago and evolved over time. We combined the two historic architectural styles of Ojai—one more Mediterranean and the other more agrarian—to help us achieve our goal. We used antique building materials, including reclaimed antique French terra-cotta roof tiles and vintage barn beams and cupolas, as well as antique limestone fireplace mantels and wood doors, all of which brought their own sense of history to our home.

The historic nature of our home is juxtaposed with a sense of modernity. Unframed sheets of glass in our bedroom nurture a connection to the gardens. There are no decorative trims or moldings except those from Giannetti Studio that are on display in our hallway as an homage to my family heritage. Our steel windows also recall the industrial design that I've loved since childhood. In contrast to the broken-up spaces in older historic homes, Patina Farm has an open floor plan, where the public rooms flow together.

To embrace a sense of calm, we limited the palette to a few neutral tones. White plaster, grayed cedar planks and limestone washed in a pale linen-colored grout cover the walls. The flooring materials are confined to a bleached white French oak and creamy French limestone. Inspired by the gardens, the furnishings palette is also neutral and includes textured natural linens, aged leather and verdant antique textiles. Nothing is precious. These selections give our rooms a sense of comfortable tranquility, where our friends and family are invited to relax.

ABOVE: A collection of ornamental plaster pieces from Giannetti Studio is an homage to my family history. The decorative screen on the wall is a flea market find from years ago that embodies our Patina Style design philosophy. RIGHT: Our elegant Belgian verdure tapestry and worn leather chairs are the perfect combination of rustic and refined.

LEFT: Instead of a traditional dining room, we placed our dining table in the center of our home between the front and back steel doors, making it more versatile and connecting it to the gardens. ABOVE: Another display of Giannetti Studio plaster pieces adds a chalky patina to the wall between our dining and kitchen.

ABOVE: A collection of Giannetti Studio wood and metal molds are displayed above a black Swedish cabinet in our son Nick's room. RIGHT: A two-sided limestone fireplace is the only separation between our dining-living room and our kitchen. Two of our "Kate" chairs and a continental-height, antique, oval table by the fire makes a cozy breakfast room.

Provençal

*W*hat do you do when a couple comes to you and they have differing ideas for the type of home they want? That was the challenge we faced when designing this home. The wife loved classic French design, while the husband was drawn to modern architecture. The result is a beautiful property that is both Provençal and modern. In the rooms where the wife spends more time, the aesthetic leans more feminine and French. In the spaces where the husband spends more of his time, we used more modern detailing.

A cohesive palette of creamy Texas limestone, white plaster, and warm white oak creates a consistent aesthetic throughout the spaces. Shades of gray are added as an accent: a light blue-gray in her rooms and a darker steel-gray in his.

The other design challenge was the balance of public and private spaces. Our clients wanted their home to include more formal rooms, allowing them to have large parties and events, but they also wanted to create a home that was comfortable for their family of four. In order to meet both of these needs, we placed the formal living room and dining room in the front of the house. A series of steel French doors can be opened to the front patios and gardens, enlarging these public spaces for bigger events. In the center of the home, a glassed-in stairway has the air of a European central courtyard, bringing light into the home and also separating the public spaces from the more intimate family rooms.

Our clients also wanted a home that supported an indoor-outdoor lifestyle. Similar to the formal rooms at the front of the house, the family room, breakfast room, and kitchen are open to the gardens in the back of the house. A wall of steel doors pocket to connect the family room to the covered porch, enlarging the space and providing views of the pool and the stone-covered guesthouse. Tall, steel French doors connect the breakfast room to a rose-covered sitting area and the outdoor barbecue.

When their home was complete, our clients told us it felt just like them. That's always our goal.

LEFT: Potted cypress, olive and boxwood surround the carved limestone fountain in the stair hall. ABOVE: Light pours into the stairway through a set of south-facing, two-story glass windows. Exterior-style wall lanterns on a limestone wall and large limestone floor pavers give the stairway a feeling of being an exterior courtyard. OVERLEAF: Hand-painted wall paneling in pale shades of blue-gray provides a feeling of enclosure to the formal living room. An antique French limestone mantel is the focal point to the room and also adds a bit of rusticity.

LEFT: Accent pillows made from an antique tapestry and the same celadon velvet that is used in the dining room visually connect the formal living and dining spaces. ABOVE: Dining chairs are upholstered in a celadon green, complementing the hand-painted wall mural.

ABOVE: Steel-framed windows and door give a glimpse into the kitchen pantry. RIGHT: The tall, arched, steel doors and a nature-inspired color palette give the breakfast room a garden room aesthetic.

LEFT: Warm, stained-oak-paneled walls are paired with cooler toned gray cashmere draperies and upholstery in his office. A Giannetti "George" chair, upholstered in soft black leather, and a planetary photo with a black background add some strength to the palette. ABOVE: Although the basement powder room has the same color palette, the simpler detailing of the stone sink and the industrial lighting and plumbing fixtures give this room a more modern ambience.

ABOVE: The upstairs sitting area walls and ceiling are painted a deep blue-green to create a cozy space for reading or watching TV. RIGHT: A Dennis and Leen tall cabinet with a blue-green finish is located in the upstairs hallway across from an olive tree in a cream-colored cement planter from Elegant Earth.

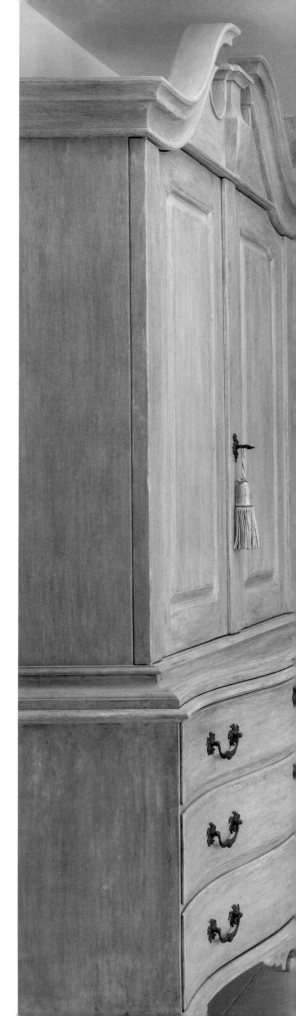

ABOVE: A mirrored lantern from Urban Electric hangs in the center of the stone wine cellar. Lighting inside the wine storage gives the entire room a glow. RIGHT: A ficus tree is planted in a large stone planter at the bottom of the basement stairway. One of our clients' favorite Metallica quotes is written in gold leaf on the sliding glass door in the bar.

EXIT LIGHT
ENTER NIGHT
TAKE MY HAND
WE'RE OFF TO
NEVER-NEVER LAND

LEFT: The basement of the home has a more modern feel, to reflect the husband's taste. It uses the same palette of oak, stone and plaster to visually unify the home. ABOVE: The movie theatre is outfitted in charcoal mohair with charcoal linen walls, which provides a muted background for the images on-screen. We used brass studs on the wall upholstery and tables to recall vintage travel trunks.

ABOVE AND RIGHT: The guest cottage houses a bedroom on the second floor and a sitting room on the ground level, overlooking the pool. The steel bifold doors by Riviera open on all sides to create an open porch. The cottage is designed in a more rustic style that mixes in a modern sensibility.

Atherton

Atherton reflects the stories and dream of our clients. They raised their family in a beautiful traditional home on this tree-filled property, but their children were older now. They were entering a new phase of their life and their house no longer fit their lifestyle. They dreamed of open interior spaces, where they could entertain friends and their grown children. After seeing Patina Farm, they were convinced they could create a home that reminded them of their original, traditional house but also included bright, fluid spaces connected to their gardens.

I reinterpreted the scale of traditional architectural elements to give the structure a more modern aesthetic. Monumental, four-by-eight-foot double-hung windows also brought more light into the spaces. I used simplified versions of classical details—flat siding instead of shiplap and tall, pale-gray steel windows with unadorned bronze lever handles—to add a more industrial feel to the house. A mix of metal standing-seam and slate roofs breaks up the massing, making the house feel like a series of separate buildings.

Although the interior rooms have a modern sensibility, I also wanted them to feel warm and welcoming. A few antique architectural elements—a large-scale limestone mantel in the living room, a pair of antique French pine doors in the breakfast room, and two vintage zinc industrial pendants in the kitchen—help balance the contemporary detailing. The view of the gardens through the generous steel windows becomes large-scale landscape art, adding a natural ease to the interior spaces.

In contrast to our clients' original house, the rooms in their new home flow together. The dining room connects to the spacious living room to create a generous place for entertaining, and the kitchen, breakfast and family rooms join to make one large gathering space, perfect for the way our clients enjoy living now.

LEFT: An antique gilt mirror and two of my paintings are displayed on the antique French limestone mantel with a simple arrangement of branches cut from the garden. ABOVE: The living room furnishings are a mix of Swedish and industrial antiques, adding a rusticity to the modern sense of space. Two of our Giannetti "Alix" sofas are slipcovered in an ivory linen and adorned with antiqued velvet and silk pillows.

ABOVE: Located next to the kitchen, this family room is where our clients hang out. The expansive steel windows turn the space into an extension of the garden. A large hanging lantern, a Japanese maple tree in the corner and natural, neutral fabrics and materials add to the outdoor aesthetic. RIGHT: A limited palette of plant materials—white floribunda roses, clipped boxwood and birch and maple trees—adds a calmness to the exterior.

LEFT: Wicker chairs and a natural wood table create an outdoor aesthetic in the breakfast room. We used a pair of antique pine doors for the pantry. ABOVE: Cantilevered marble shelves flank a large steel window. A pair of vintage zinc industrial lights from Elizabeth Taylor's tennis court (a tribute to our client's father's history with the actress) hang over the island.

LEFT: A collection of antique books and coral are on display in a black Swedish cabinet in the living room. ABOVE: An ornately carved mirror is paired with a clean, modern cement sink in the powder room.

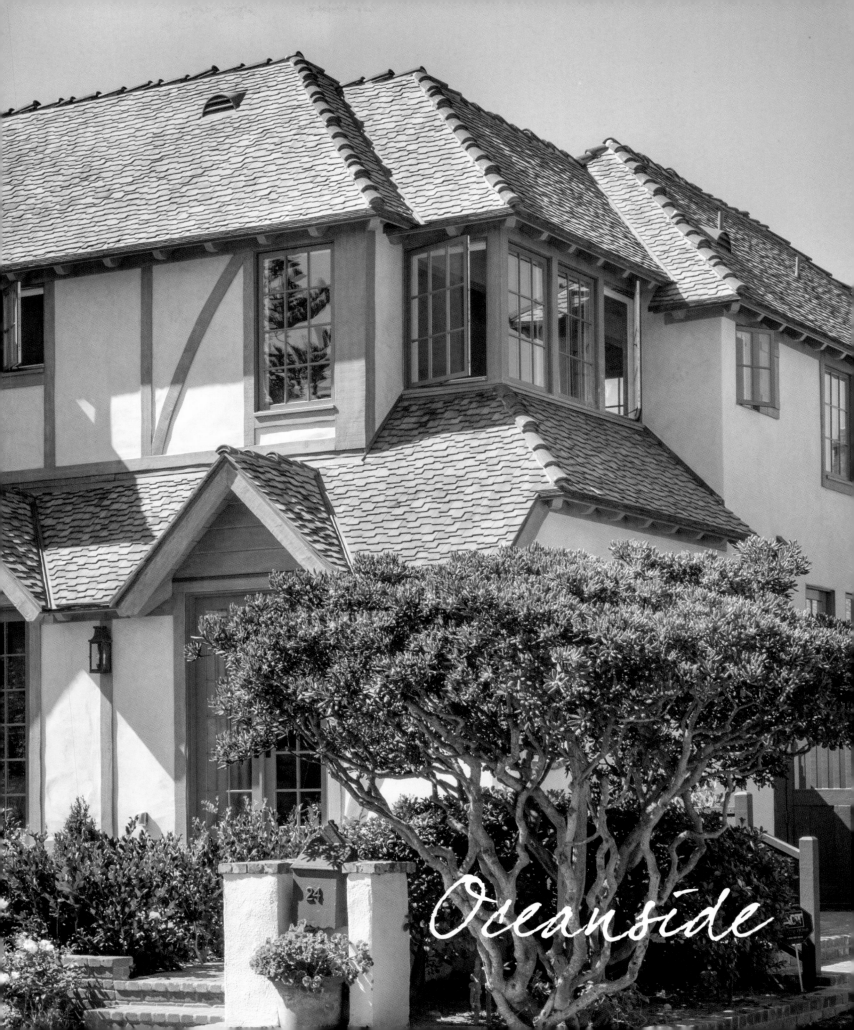

Oceanside

Oceanside is a home in a private beach enclave in Southern California. Built in the 1920s, all of the houses in this community are based on classic French Normandy architecture, and all new homes are required to adhere to these details.

Our clients' dream was to build a home where they could provide their own children with the same kind of carefree summers in the same beach community that they visited during their own childhoods. They imagined a home that would feel comfortable when it was just the two of them but was also expandable to a multigenerational compound.

With these primary objectives, I designed a French Normandy–style home centered around a courtyard, where the living room, dining room and kitchen flow together and connect to a porch with spectacular ocean views. Combined with our clients' bedroom suite, these spaces become a comfortable two-person home. As more guests arrive, the extra bedrooms and bunk room surrounding the courtyard extend the home while still protecting our clients' privacy.

High-pitched roofs, dormers, a courtyard turret, and brick and timber detailing ensure the exterior of the home blends in with the rest of the charming residences in the neighborhood. But the interior architecture reveals this house's modern side. Tall, twenty-foot pitched ceilings and the liberal use of windows and glass doors give the living room an undeniable present-day aesthetic. Minimal trims and a limited neutral palette of materials were used in order to keep the interiors uncluttered. Pared-down versions of traditional light fixtures were also selected. All of these design decisions created fresh, modern spaces that still reminded our clients of their childhood memories.

ABOVE: A pair of wood-plank doors provide privacy for the interior courtyard. Brick Gothic archways were inspired by the Normandy details of the original homes in the community. RIGHT: We created a cozy seating area in front of the fireplace for our clients to enjoy on those chilly coastal evenings. A round table surrounded by wicker chairs is an intimate dining option, protected from the ocean wind.

ABOVE: In the living room, a collection of glass Japanese fishing floats and a model sailboat are placed on top of the antique French limestone mantel. RIGHT: An island surrounded with barstools and wicker seating around a long, antique farm table provide ample seating for entertaining. OVERLEAF LEFT: A wood countertop on a section of kitchen cabinetry painted Farrow and Ball French Gray gives it the appearance of furniture. OVERLEAF RIGHT: A wood island with a sink and a white Calacatta marble countertop provide extra prep areas in the center of the kitchen. The second island separates the kitchen from the dining room.

ABOVE: Located off the kitchen, a cozy family room with a palette inspired by the ocean is a more intimate space for our clients to relax together or with their children. RIGHT: A handmade metal fish, part of the weather vane on the original house on the property, adds a little history to our clients' new home.

LEFT: In the bedroom, a pair of chairs and a matching ottoman upholstered in a soft, durable outdoor fabric provide a cozy interlude in front of an antique French limestone mantel. A beautiful vintage rug in shades of ocean blue and taupes grounds the space. ABOVE: A gilt barometer, a collection of bleached coral and vintage books add texture and interest.

LEFT: In the bathroom we paired antiqued limestone pavers in random widths on the floor with honed, white marble slabs on the walls to create a spalike atmosphere. Next to the freestanding bathtub, two side tables provide a place for towels and soaps. ABOVE: A bedside table with an open shelf allows for extra blanket and pillow storage in the bedroom.

ABOVE: Built-in storage and nautical-inspired lighting give the bunkroom a ship aesthetic. RIGHT: A pair of vintage ship blueprints hang above an industrial table holding a collection of ship models. A pair of vintage champagne crates are repurposed into seating as well as storage for this guest room.

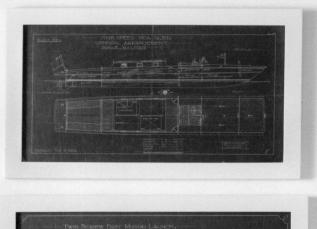

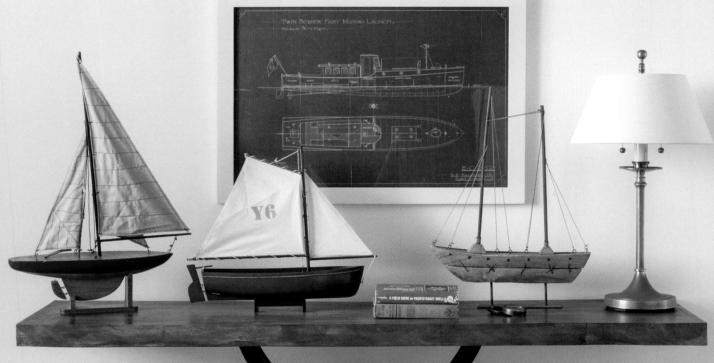

LEFT: Window seats in a couple of the larger guest rooms work double duty as extra sleeping/napping nooks.
ABOVE: A skylight in this guest shower allows the light to pour in while still maintaining privacy. Pretty, natural baskets on the shelves of a custom open sink base, painted Farrow and Ball French Gray, allow for extra towel storage.

Maine

*M*aine is the realization of my client's wish to create a multigenerational family retreat inspired by the local Maine architecture, her father's love of wooden boat building and her own affection for modern design.

The bayside property includes a larger, gambrel-roof main house and a smaller, post-and-beam barn guesthouse. From the exterior, both structures appear to have existed on the property for generations. It is upon entering the homes that guests are welcomed to the open spaces with the feel of a more contemporary design. The interior shell of the house was simplified with natural plaster walls and no decorative moldings. I selected clean, modern architectural details for kitchen and bathroom cabinetry as well as contemporary plumbing fixtures for these rooms. A limited palette of materials allows the rooms to flow together visually.

Several of the interior details pay respect to my client's father's appreciation for the craftsmanship of the local boat builders. The joinery in the oak beams was emphasized, and I used common boat detailing for the interior tongue-and-groove wood walls. In several of the bedrooms, walls of built-in cabinetry adorned with leather handles give the rooms an air of a boat cabin.

The connection to local Maine architecture was of utmost importance. All materials, including the stained oak flooring and beams as well as the soapstone and granite in the kitchens and bathrooms, were locally sourced. My client filled the home with unique pieces found in local antique shops. We designed custom upholstered furniture pieces in a scale that complemented the antiques but also added a little modern twist to the interiors.

This home was an exercise in how to borrow from both architectural and cultural history, imbuing an emotional weight to design elements by having them made by members of the community and become an homage to an individual.

PREVIOUS OVERLEAF: A pair of vintage leather chairs and a natural linen–slipcovered Giannetti "Courtney" sofa are located in the main living room. The mantel is made from locally sourced granite. Rough-hewn beams are juxtaposed to the more modern, detailed wood-plank wall.

RIGHT: Modern detailing, plumbing fixtures and hardware were used in the kitchen.

ABOVE: The powder room was fully paneled in wood to create the feeling of being onboard a ship. Green soapstone slabs were locally sourced. RIGHT: A set of Giannetti "Frasier" chairs are set around a zinc-top table in the open living-dining area. OVERLEAF: An octagonal sitting room off the kitchen takes full advantage of the magnificent views of the bay.

ABOVE: A pair of Giannetti "Nate" chairs in front of built-in oak bookcases becomes a cozy reading nook on the stair landing. RIGHT: An oak timber truss celebrates the work of local craftsmen. A second-story deck is a superb place for enjoying the view of boats in the bay. OVERLEAF: In the main bedroom, the low sill of the large, arched window accentuates the connection to the landscape. The built-in oak shelves and desk give the space a stateroom aesthetic.

LEFT: A window seat in one of the guest rooms provides an additional sleeping nook with a view of the bay. ABOVE: All the secondary bathrooms have a palette of local soapstone slabs and oak paneling.

LEFT: : The living room was furnished using local antiques, including this charming safe now repurposed as a side table between two vintage leather chairs.

ABOVE: My first sketch of Maine showing the barn and the house. These early sketches often catch the essence of the final design.

PREVIOUS OVERLEAF: Massive stones found on the site were placed in the landscape to visually connect the guest and main houses. LEFT: Retractable screens allow the deck to be used year-round and provide uninterrupted flow from the house. ABOVE: The guest barn houses a bedroom and bunk room as well as a kitchen and a two-story dining room.

LEFT: The guesthouse kitchen, with one of my paintings above the stove. ABOVE: The dining area features Giannetti "Leila" chairs and a custom industrial sash light fixture. OVERLEAF: The post-and-beam construction of the guest "barn" is left exposed. Vertical wood columns separate the living room from the dining area.

Cliff House

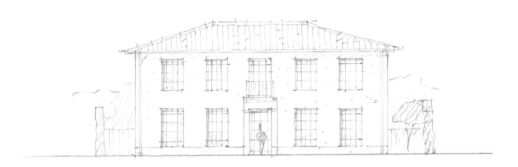

This Malibu home, equal parts industrial factory and Italian villa, is a departure from the traditional shingle-style beach house I designed for this same client a decade ago. His old house became the set for the TV show *Grace and Frankie*. When my client sold the original house, he contacted me and was ready to experience the beach in a new way, which could only be had by designing a completely different type of home.

One of my main goals was to connect the indoor spaces to the ocean beyond. I wanted to take advantage of this home's location on a cliff above the Pacific. From the entry courtyard, a steel-and-glass door allows visitors a peek at the magnificent views. Upon entering the house, monumental steel doors pocket into the wall, providing guests with the full, breathtaking sights, scents and sounds of the ocean. The entire home becomes an outdoor porch.

The natural materials—oak on the stairs and walls, sand-colored limestone and antique terra-cotta roof tiles—bring warmth to the house. Hand-troweled plaster walls have the feeling of craft, sculpture, and a connection to the earth. The sun hitting the plaster ceiling makes it shimmer like the ocean. The polished cement floors are a reminder of Giannetti Studio and my industrial heritage.

Throughout the house, I use classical proportions in an industrial vernacular. On the front facade of the house, I use a ratio called the golden section—the proportions of classical beauty—for all of the steel window mullions. This proportion is echoed on a larger scale on the ocean side of the house to dramatize the twelve-foot ceilings. My client's home was an opportunity to create an exciting new style of architecture and to explore the confluence of industrial details, modern use of space and classical proportions.

PREVIOUS OVERLEAF: When the steel doors are open, the entire home becomes connected to the outdoors. Hidden roll-down shades soften the afternoon sun.

RIGHT: In the kitchen, a two-story oak-paneled element hides the pantry and appliances. The wave-shaped plaster hood above the range adds a little curve to the more linear elements.

ABOVE AND RIGHT: The steel windows on the front of the home are echoed in a much larger scale in the breakfast room. The golden section proportions tie the elements together visually.

PREVIOUS OVERLEAF: The master bedroom has a wall of glass that opens to a large roof deck overlooking the Pacific.

RIGHT: The shower and water-closet spaces become sandblasted glass-and-steel lanterns in the master bath.

ABOVE AND RIGHT: The guesthouse, across the courtyard from the main house, brings in the industrial aesthetic with the board-formed concrete retaining walls left exposed. OVERLEAF: The massive pocket doors provide a connection to the patio and a view of the coast. Steel trellises covered in willow provide a shady retreat.

Palm Desert

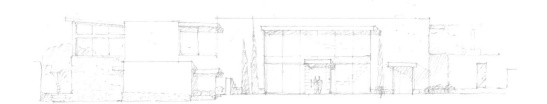

Several years ago, one of my clients reached out to me. He had purchased a beautiful piece of land in Palm Desert with magnificent views of the Santa Rosa Mountains. He wanted to create a modern house that would take advantage of the temperate fall and winter climate. He asked me for recommendations of architects who specialized in modern architecture, and I was happy to share my thoughts on who would be a great match. A few weeks later, the client called again to update me about who he had chosen. He had interviewed the architects and was concerned that they might make the house too cold and uninviting. He said he knew I could create a modern home with the warmth of the project I had designed for him previously. He congratulated me on being chosen to design his new home!

As I began the design process, I was reminded of a drawing in one of my travel sketchbooks that I had done more than thirty years prior on a trip to Paris. The sketch was of a very modern space. The walls were painted drywall and the flooring was a simple tile. Although I was drawn to the modern sense of space, the materials felt dull and lifeless. Next to the sketch I had written, "Is it possible to create a modern space with more earthy materials? Explore when I get home." It only took me thirty-five years to finally take this idea to the next level.

I gathered the same palette that we used at Patina Farm—creamy limestone, light-white oak, white plaster, and pale-gray steel windows—and applied it to a truly indoor-outdoor contemporary home. I poured over the work of modern masters Neutra, Schindler, and Mies for inspiration. I designed the home as a series of pavilions linked together by glassed-in passages, interwoven with courtyards and a reflecting pool. I wanted the landscape to pass through the house.

Plaster walls and limestone flooring continue from the inside to the outside, and doors made of twelve-foot-tall glass panels retract into the walls, blurring the line between indoor and outdoor spaces. These details also create a feeling of weightlessness, where the oak ceilings float high above and it feels as if the stairway is levitating in the landscape.

BELOW: My sketch from 1984 of the Maison La Roche Jeanneret served as inspiration for the living-dining room.

RIGHT: The view of the Santa Rosa Mountains upon entering.

OVERLEAF: A wooden bridge connects the second-floor portions of the home.

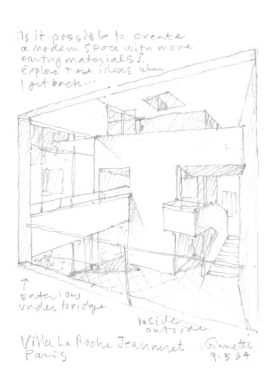

Is it possible to create
a modern space with more
earthy materials?
Explore these ideas when
I get back...

Enter low
under bridge

inside
outside

Villa La Roche Jeanneret   Gionetti
Paris   9.5.84

Lucky

THE MIRÓ EYE
Ellsworth Kelly

PREVIOUS OVERLEAF: The stair is treated like modern sculpture to complement the owner's art collection.

LEFT: A game room wing of the home hosts a bowling alley, billiards table and screening room.

OVERLEAF: The family room features a beautiful sunburst bar designed by Busta Studio.

PREVIOUS OVERLEAF: The master bedroom connects seamlessly to the garden with walls of retractable glass.

RIGHT: The home flows into the landscape designed by Sammy Castro. The glass walls of the house retract and connect to the sculpture garden and a zero-edge pool.

OVERLEAF: In the evening, fiber-optic lighting in the pool echoes the star-filled night sky.

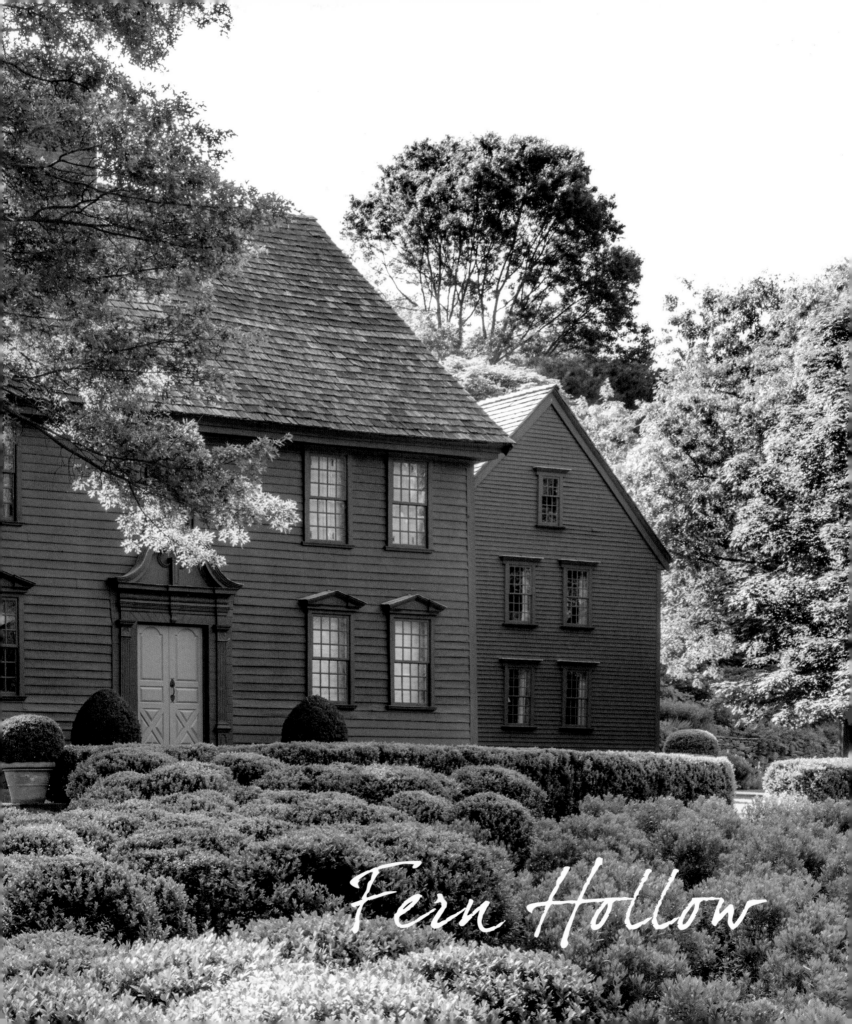

Fern Hollow

We were given the ambitious commission to renovate and reimagine the interior design of this graceful historic home in bucolic Litchfield County, Connecticut. Five antique structures, ranging from a 17th-century iron monger's home to an 18th-century historically significant house, were assembled into a unique, sprawling estate. Our clients felt a sense of stewardship toward this authentic architecture and had originally designed the interior to match the period. Years later, they felt the interior no longer reflected who they were or how they wanted to live.

With each architectural decision I made during the renovation—whether it was the addition of antique wood shelving in the library, creating a wine room in the cellar or designing a closet in the attic using antique lumber—I wanted to honor the work of the original craftspeople.

We also wanted to add a calmer, modern feel to the interior design. We reimagined the interior by simplifying the color palette, using Farrow and Ball Pavilion Gray for all the wood wall paneling and Farrow and Ball Wimborne White for the walls, a sunny white that reflects the outside light, making the rooms feel brighter. We updated all the light fixtures, which had felt very dated. Using cleaner, modern fixtures and editing the furnishings gave us the ability to see the stunning architecture.

We incorporated the homeowners' cherished antiques to keep their memories intact and repositioned their collections into groups, giving them more of an impact. We replaced old, bulky, chintz-covered upholstery with clean-lined, natural-linen upholstery, a lovely juxtaposition to the more formal English and Swedish antiques. Removing many of the area rugs allowed the impressively wide, original pine flooring to be appreciated, and we switched out other, floral-patterned hooked rugs with visually soothing natural fiber selections.

It's often more about what you take away than it is about adding more. Especially when the house has a history and natural beauty, it's best to simply respect the integrity of the house.

ABOVE: A pair of wood doors in the two-story music room open to reveal the lush gardens that surround the home. Natural-linen sofas and a pair of bergère chairs are adorned with pillows in greens and neutrals that connect with the gardens.
RIGHT: An ornate gilt mirror hangs above a Swedish settee upholstered in a taupe silk velvet. Natural-linen draperies on silver leaf rods frame the views. We replaced the large floral tapestry rug with a natural woven rug to create a sense of calm.

LEFT: Originally stained dark brown, the existing heavy timbers were bleached to complement the color scheme in the rest of the house and to make them feel visually lighter. Painting the paneling in the house a lighter color of gray also made the beautiful details more prominent. ABOVE: A tall Swedish clock was placed at the bottom of the stair leading to the guest rooms. OVERLEAF: Plaster pieces from Giannetti Studio are on display with a collection of our clients' first-edition volumes. Painting the original wood paneling Farrow and Ball Pavilion Gray brings out the details.

ABOVE AND RIGHT: We removed the rug from the dining room to expose the impressive, wide-plank pine floors. All of the wood trim, cabinetry and ceiling beams were stripped, revealing the beauty of the natural wood.

PREVIOUS OVERLEAF: The furnishings in the family kitchen are the perfect example of rustic and ornate. A set of finely carved Swedish chairs are paired with a more provincial farm table. A pair of Giannetti "Kate" chairs are upholstered in a natural linen for a comfortable place to enjoy breakfast. **ABOVE:** A charming, diminutive window shines light into the small powder room vestibule. **RIGHT:** We added shelves made from antique lumber to turn this cozy space into a proper library. Leather-upholstered Giannetti "Clive" wing chairs provide seating by the two antique desks, allowing our client to peruse his collection of historic literature. A sitting area is comprised of Giannetti furniture pieces, slipcovered in natural linen, surrounding a Giannetti "Mason" ottoman in saddle-colored leather.

ABOVE: A Swedish altar piece is surrounded by garden elements. RIGHT: We gathered our clients' impressive collection of blue-and-white china to create a dramatic display in the entry hall. OVERLEAF: We brought together our clients' collection of black antique ladder-back chairs and paired them with the dark-stained highboy to add strength to this sitting room outside our client's office. A Giannetti "Clive" chair, upholstered in natural linen, adds some softness to the space.

LEFT: I converted the attic into a master closet by adding antique beams and linen drapery to obscure the clothing. Custom cabinetry, cove lighting and a few Swedish benches were added to complete the room. ABOVE: A modern sink in the powder room contrasts with a beautiful gilt mirror.

LEFT: The guest room uses a neutral palette of natural linens. ABOVE: The guest bath vanity is custom made from old oak beams. OVERLEAF: A wine cellar was created in the basement using antique beams and racks. Giannetti slipcovered "Frasier" chairs surround a tasting table.

Bonhill

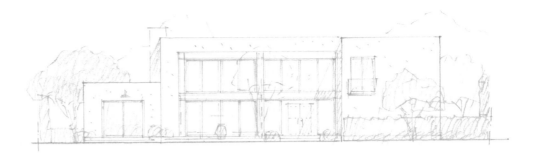

Bonhill is an exciting collaboration with repeat clients who always bring their personal sense of style to the design of their homes. Their distinctive taste comes from their history of renovating and living in an old vicarage in the English countryside as well as residing in an industrial loft in London. They wanted to bring some of their personal architectural story into their new home. The result is a singular design where the structural steel frame is left exposed, to be appreciated as a thing of beauty, and the patina of vintage elements is elevated to art.

Although my clients loved the strength and modernity the two-story steel added to their house, they also wanted their home to feel rustic and warm. To achieve this, we paired the steel with several antique architectural elements. Vintage timber trusses and reclaimed floor planks add an air of a bygone garret. A pair of zinc industrial fire doors are refashioned as the front entrance, and a monumental megaphone is repurposed as a light fixture in the entry. The entire house design is a series of juxtapositions: the relationship of modern steel and glass with rustic woods, the balance between a neutral architectural palette and vibrant artwork and furnishings.

While bringing their unique British history to their home, my clients also appreciated the location of the property and wanted the design to take advantage of the temperate Los Angeles climate. Oversized two-story walls of glass connected the interiors to the landscape. Large steel-framed glass doors allowed the garden to flow through the house from front to back. The plant palette was limited so that the exterior did not compete with the vibrant colors of the furnishings.

This home is unlike any I had designed before. There were times during the design process where it felt like we were on a tightwire, balancing all of these different design elements. It was incredibly satisfying to view what my clients and I had achieved. It was a lesson in trust for all involved, and that trust paid off in the end.

LEFT: I exposed an existing brick fireplace to enhance the loft aesthetic and become another piece of artwork on the wall.
ABOVE: Monumental antique columns are a large-scale balancing element in the space. OVERLEAF: The kitchen was designed using classic English Country design details, reflecting the clients' heritage.

Wisteria

Although our clients had owned this home in Santa Monica for twenty years, it wasn't until a few years ago that they decided to turn this dark bungalow into a light-filled cottage that connected to the gardens. The size of their home often limited our clients' ability to entertain and the number of people they could accommodate. We were able to enlarge their home by connecting the inside spaces to the outdoors.

The kitchen was totally redone to include an industrial-inspired steel island and cantilevered marble shelves for accessible storage. A wall of beautiful decorative tile in the same blues and grays that we used in the rest of the home created a focal point in the kitchen. We replaced the small wood window over the sink with a steel window for a view of the back garden and potager.

Off the kitchen and dining room, we replaced small wood French doors with larger, pale-gray–blue steel doors that allow the eye to focus on the lovely outdoor dining area. Dappled light flows through the canopy of trees we planted below the raised deck. We replaced the dark fencing and wooden deck floor with chalky-gray scaffolding planks, adding patina to the space.

Increasing the light to all the rooms and connecting them to the outside were two priorities. We added another set of large French doors to the master bedroom, which allowed the morning light to fill the space. Just outside these doors, a comfortable seating area by an outdoor fireplace is protected by a rose-covered trellis, providing a gorgeous view as well as expanding the size of the bedroom.

The family room also got a new set of French doors. The same neutral color palette was used on both indoor and outdoor seating areas to allow these spaces to flow and to blur the lines between indoors and outdoors.

We renovated the gardens to combine structure and romance. Boxwood clipped into spheres and small hedges add formality and are juxtaposed with the more naturalistic wisteria and rose vines. A David Austin Rose garden in the back provides a breathtaking focal point while allowing a peek into the lush vegetable garden beyond.

227

LEFT: New steel doors open the dining room to the outdoor deck for expanded entertaining space. **ABOVE:** We were able to save the mature rose vines while replacing the old arbor. We added a brick fireplace to create a cozy outdoor seating area.

ABOVE: We painted the cabinetry Farrow and Ball Cornforth, a pale-gray hue that picks up the cool-gray tones in the Calacatta marble countertops. RIGHT: A decorative tile by Walker Zanger becomes a focal point in the neutral kitchen.

LEFT: The stainless steel island and appliances add an industrial aesthetic to the space. ABOVE: Cantilevered marble shelves provide a place for open display and storage. OVERLEAF: In the main bedroom, we added large French doors to connect it to the backyard seating area and to allow light to flow into the room.

Creekside

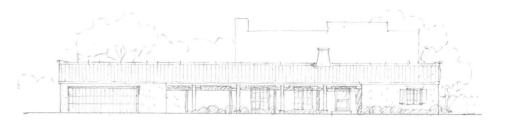

The owners of this Creekside home in Malibu contacted us after seeing Patina Farm featured in *Veranda* magazine. The wife wanted to brighten up and calm down the existing Spanish-style house and was drawn to the light, neutral palette of our home. Her husband wasn't convinced—until they came for a visit. We met them at our gate and the husband explained that he liked the existing dark wood floors and beams as well as the deep burnt-orange terra-cotta tiles of their creek-side abode. Then he stepped into our home, with its bleached oak and creamy limestone floors, bright white walls and pale-gray steel doors and windows, and I could see his body relax. "I love it. Do whatever you want," he said.

There were several architectural changes that we made to the house in order to achieve the calm, airy aesthetic our clients desired. We replaced the short, dark-wood French doors with taller, slimmer, lighter steel windows and doors, which allowed more light to flow in and also connected the interiors to the garden. In the living room and kitchen, we painted the dark-wood ceilings white and bleached the beams to open up the height of the spaces. We also opened up the stairway, making the main living space feel more expansive. The ornate stair railing was replaced with simple iron pickets with a small knuckle detail. The dark, shiny wood floor was replaced with a lighter European oak floor in a relaxed, rustic finish.

Similar to Patina Farm, we added a few antique doors to balance the more modern details in the house. We also used charming rustic antique furniture pieces as sink bases paired with cleaner lined plumbing fixtures in unlacquered brass.

The furnishing selections are also a balance of modern and rustic. Giannetti Home upholstery in natural linen is adorned with warm-hued textile pillows. A selection of European casual antiques in light finishes and pale area rugs provide texture and interest in the spaces.

When we completed this project, our client called to say how happy she and her husband were with all of the changes and how they felt relaxed when they spent time at their Malibu home. I reminded her of their first visit to Patina Farm and her husband's reaction to our house. We both laughed. Yes, that visit was very convincing.

239

ABOVE: The sitting area uses our "Nick" chairs and ottomans along with a few Swedish antiques to create a cozy area.
RIGHT: The kitchen connects to the breakfast area. Giannetti "Frasier" and "Leila" chairs surround the breakfast table.

LEFT: A Giannetti "Clive" chair sits at our "Rochelle" desk. ABOVE: The home was furnished with our Giannetti Home furniture and Swedish antiques. OVERLEAF LEFT: A sheet of glass creates an uninterrupted garden view. OVERLEAF RIGHT: A modern sculptural bathtub and sinks were selected to balance the more rustic antique sink base in this bathroom.

PREVIOUS OVERLEAF LEFT: Antique Chicago brick lining the firebox is paired with a modern plaster mantel. PREVIOUS OVERLEAF RIGHT: An antique Swedish secretaire becomes as a bedside table and desk. A slipcovered Giannetti "Frasier" chair can be pulled up to the desk or moved by the fireplace. ABOVE: The master sinks are custom cabinets made to look like antiques. RIGHT: The bathtub sits in an arched niche with plaster walls. Recessed motorized drapes provide privacy.

Fonplegade

Fonplegade is a beautiful historic chateau and biodynamic winery located in the Bordeaux region of France. When our clients contacted us, they were just finishing the extensive restoration of the property and were ready to focus on the interior decorating. Using our clients' passion for the land and their love of relaxed indoor-outdoor living as inspiration, we began to make plans for the interiors.

We faced the task of creating interiors that complemented the formal architecture of the chateau balanced with our clients' desire to live in spaces that were comfortable and inviting to family and guests. To achieve this goal, we chose tailored pieces upholstered in a less formal natural linen. We used draperies in the same textured linen, with a matching tape to add some detail. In the entry, we hung ornate gilt frames with antique mirrors that were the perfect balance of formality and rusticity.

We also used garden elements inside the chateau to visually connect to the garden as well as add some informality to the indoor spaces. In the dining room, we juxtaposed a pair of trees in oversized zinc planters with the more formal rock crystal chandelier that hung over the dining table. Moss-covered garden elements were positioned in many of the other rooms, as well as potted boxwood. We clipped branches from the oak trees and cut flowers from the garden instead of using formal floral arrangements. Pillows made from verdure tapestry remnants adorn many of the sofas and chairs, creating a color palette inspired by nature.

When we completed the installation, our clients said the chateau now feels like their home but also feels like it is part of the land. That was the best compliment they could have given us.

LEFT: A simple arrangement of oak branches cut from the property is on display on top of a stone console in the entry. Other stone garden elements add to the garden aesthetic. ABOVE: A pair of stone-topped demilunes and tall gilt mirrors flank the front door in the entry.

ABOVE: Olive trees in large zinc planters add greenery to the formal dining room. A vibrant piece of artwork hangs in the space, adding a modern touch. RIGHT: An oversized terra-cotta garden element is placed next to a diminutive child's bergère chair, giving a playful sense of scale to the formal living room.

A four-poster bed, upholstered in natural linen, adds some height to one of the bedrooms. A natural woven rug, quilted linen, and tapestry pillows provide texture in the calm, neutral space.

Malibu Colony

This Malibu Colony beach house was my opportunity to create the perfect beach house by having every single element conform to the single purpose of opening the whole space to the ocean.

The biggest design challenge was making the home feel spacious given the small lot size. Although this beach-front property has spectacular views, the house could be only twenty-six feet wide. The interior side walls are covered in bright white plaster to make the spaces feel more expansive. Facing the ocean views, walls of tall glass doors on both the ground level and the second floor slide away, opening the interior spaces to the outdoors. Sand-colored limestone, in the same warm tones as the interior oak floor, visually connects the indoors and outdoors. Pale steel windows and doors also guide the eye to the views outside.

Given the narrowness of the lot, proximity to neighbors was also an issue. I wanted the interiors to feel light while still preserving the clients' privacy. The two-story stairway became a lantern, letting light stream into the home, while the sandblasted exterior wall of glass in this space obscured the view into the home.

Although this is a contemporary house, I wanted to make sure it felt inviting. The natural material selections add warmth. Planked wood walls and floors stained a warm honey tone balance the cooler plaster and glass throughout the house. Honed slabs of buff-colored, fossilized limestone add natural texture to all of the bathrooms.

This Malibu Beach house is another example of the beautiful convergence of three design themes: classic proportions, modern sense of space and a limited palette of natural materials.

271

PREVIOUS OVERLEAF: The stair and kitchen are both paneled in oak to connect them and make them both feel larger.

RIGHT: The golden section proportions make their way into the window mullions.

All the interior walls in the building are covered in oak. The exterior walls and ceilings are plaster, to enlarge the feeling of space. A two-story window at the stair is sandblasted to let in an abundance of light but obscure the home next door.

It is with sincere gratitude that we thank the following talented people for helping us create this book:

Our dear friend Jill Cohen and her amazing associate Lizzy Hyland for their patience as they expertly guided us through the process for the fourth time! Madge Baird, our wonderful editor at Gibbs Smith, for sharing her expertise and wisdom.

Lisa Romerein for beautifully capturing our clients' homes through her lens.

Our amazing design associates, Ryan Oliva, Laura Putnam, Renata Costa, Andrew Mitchell, Nick Giannetti and Blenda Luong, for helping us turn our clients' dreams into reality.

Project Credits

Patina Farm

ARCHITECTURE: Giannetti Home
INTERIOR DESIGN: Giannetti Home
LANDSCAPE DESIGN: Giannetti Home
CONTRACTOR: Craftworks
PHOTOGRAPHY: Lisa Romerein

Atherton

ARCHITECTURE: Giannetti Home
INTERIOR DESIGN: Giannetti Home
LANDSCAPE DESIGN: Mark Porter
CONTRACTOR: Carter Seddon
PHOTOGRAPHY: Lisa Romerein

Oceanside

ARCHITECTURE: Giannetti Home
INTERIOR DESIGN: Giannetti Home
LANDSCAPE DESIGN: Giannetti Home
CONTRACTOR: Pat Dougherty
PHOTOGRAPHY: Lisa Romerein

Maine

ARCHITECTURE: Giannetti Home
INTERIOR DESIGN: Courtney Hollander
LANDSCAPE DESIGN: Bruce Riddell
CONTRACTOR: Hewes and Company
PHOTOGRAPHY: Lisa Romerein

Cliff House

ARCHITECTURE: Giannetti Home
INTERIOR DESIGN: Kathryn Queen
LANDSCAPE DESIGN: Giannetti Home
CONTRACTOR: Scott Haley
PHOTOGRAPHY: Lisa Romerein

Palm Desert

ARCHITECTURE: Giannetti Home
INTERIOR DESIGN: Busta Studio
LANDSCAPE DESIGN: Sammy Castro
CONTRACTOR: Discovery Builders
PHOTOGRAPHY: Nikolas Koenig

Fern Hollow

ARCHITECTURAL RENOVATION:
Giannetti Home
INTERIOR DESIGN: Giannetti Home
CONTRACTOR: Alan Ives
PHOTOGRAPHY: Lisa Romerein

Bonhill

ARCHITECTURE: Giannetti Home
INTERIOR DESIGN: Samantha O'Connor
LANDSCAPE DESIGN: Giannetti Home
CONTRACTOR: Morrow and Morrow
PHOTOGRAPHY: Gemma and Andrew Ingalls

Wisteria

ARCHITECTURE: Giannetti Home
INTERIOR DESIGN: Giannetti Home
LANDSCAPE DESIGN: Giannetti Home
CONTRACTOR: Jones Builder Group
PHOTOGRAPHY: Lisa Romerein

Creekside

ARCHITECTURE: Giannetti Home
INTERIOR DESIGN: Giannetti Home
LANDSCAPE DESIGN: Paul Keningale
CONTRACTOR: Jones Builder Group
PHOTOGRAPHY: Lisa Romerein

Fonplegade

INTERIOR DESIGN: Giannetti Home
PHOTOGRAPHY: Simon Upton

Malibu Colony

ARCHITECTURE: Giannetti Home
INTERIOR DESIGN: Irene Lipsey
PHOTOGRAPHY: Lisa Romerein

Provensal

ARCHITECTURE: Giannetti Home
INTERIOR DESIGN: Giannetti Home
LANDSCAPE: Giannetti Home
CONTRACTOR: Morrow and Morrow
PHOTOGRAPHY: Lisa Romerein

25 24 23 22 21   5 4 3

Published by
Gibbs Smith
P.O. Box 667
Layton, Utah 84041
1.800.835.4993 orders
www.gibbs-smith.com

Developed in collaboration with Jill Cohen Associates, LLC
Design by Rita Sowins/SOWINS DESIGN

Printed and bound in China
Gibbs Smith books are printed on either recycled, 100% post-consumer waste, FSC-certified pa-pers or on paper produced from sustainable PEFC-certified forest/controlled wood source. Learn more at www.pefc.org.

Library of Congress Cataloging-in-Publication Data

Names: Giannetti, Brooke, author. | Giannetti, Steve, author. | Romerein,   Lisa, photographer.
Title: Patina homes / Brooke Giannetti & Steve Giannetti ; principal photography by Lisa Romerein.
Description: Layton, Utah : Gibbs Smith, [2021] | Summary: "This is the first book to feature the architectural brilliance of Steve Giannetti, whose image of beauty is a place where modern, classical and industrial elements are merged to create exquisite environments enhanced with antiques and modern, refined interiors. The twelve homes showcased here were carefully crafted with a textured palette and Steve's signature materials, resulting in understated elegance. With houses ranging from modern desert to beachfront contemporary to East Coast farmhouse and a Provencal-style home in California, Steve and Brooke reveal the vision for fulfilling the dreams of any homeowner. "-- Provided by publisher.
Identifiers: LCCN 2020035582 | ISBN 9781423656845 (hardcover) | ISBN   9781423656852 (epub)
Subjects: LCSH: Giannetti, Brooke--Themes, motives. | Giannetti,
   Steve--Themes, motives. | Architecture--United States--History--21st century.
Classification: LCC NA737.G485 A4 2021 | DDC 720.973/0905--dc23
LC record available at https://lccn.loc.gov/2020035582

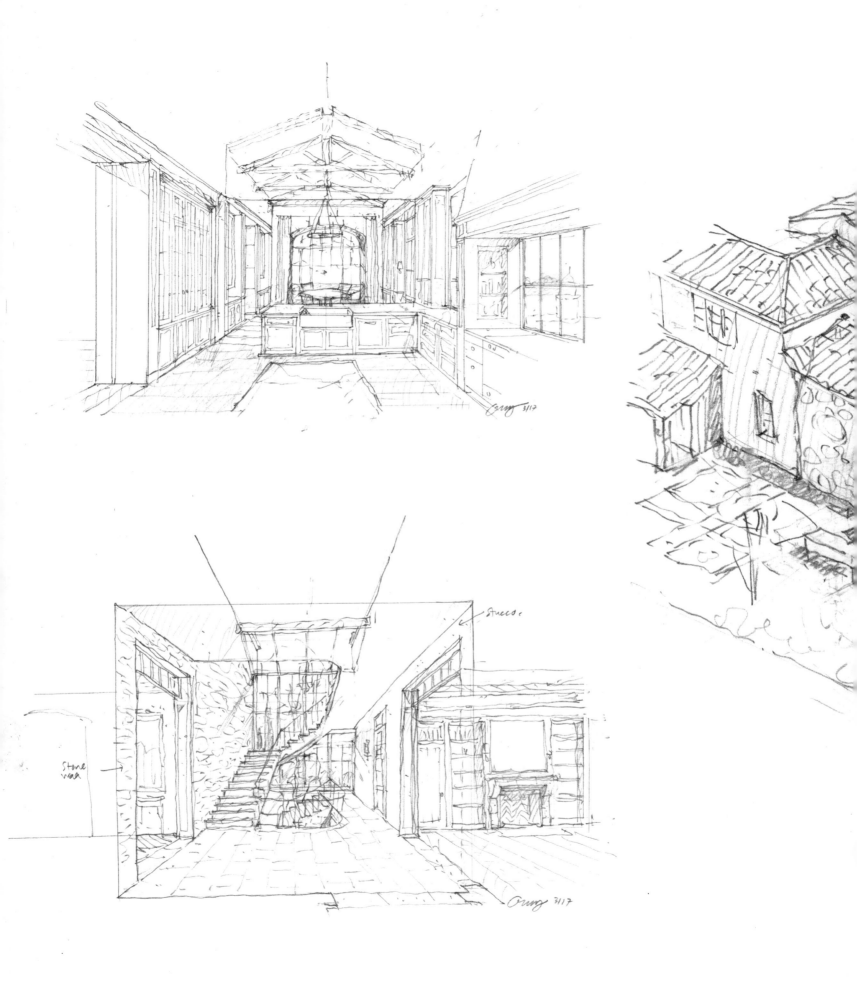

Stucco

Stone
wall

Creg 3/17

Creg 3/17